MW00583731

Hidden Scars

By: J'Naye' Wise

WRITERS REPUBLIC L.L.C.
515 Summit Ave. Unit R1
Union City, NJ 07087, USA

Website: *www.writersrepublic.com*
Hotline: *1-877-656-6838*
Email: *info@writersrepublic.com*

Ordering Information:
Quantity sales. Special discounts are available on quantity purchases by corporations, associations, and others. For details, contact the publisher at the address above.

Library of Congress Control Number: 2020946084
ISBN-13:   978-1-64620-534-9   [Paperback Edition]
                  978-1-64620-535-6   [Digital Edition]

Rev. date: 10/07/2020

Contents

Karma

We're In the boxing ring
We're playing this vicious game
We went round for round til we knocked love out
Days go by without a single sound,
How did we even get to this point,
Of who can hurt who the most
Who will have the last laugh
Shamed and belittled when our friends start to roast
There once was a time
Where I would do any and everything for you
But now im enraged, full of resentment
And cant believe what we're going through,
After the first heartache
I have you a second and third chance
I begged and pleaded that you would be a changed man,
You fucked me up mentally
Even when I moved on
I can never trust again, my faith in men is gone
Many years wasted that I can't get back
I was pregnant when you cheated
How do you live with that?
I finally built up the courage to meet you where you stand
I called the ex you hated the most

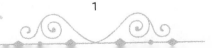

And told him I didn't have a man
"Oh two can't play your game?"
I don't understand
Lets just call it even
Before the next strike can't be un-done
Now you're scheduling dates with my friends?
You're bold ass won
Nah, I can't take that "L"
Lets go another round
I planned a last minute trip out of town
I said it was for work
To shade you from the hurt
But now you're online
Telling bitches you wanna taste them
Sending lunch money
Nah, you're playing with our income,
I'm going to end this game
Before karma gets back
Just know I really loved you
And I never meant to hurt you like that.

Drifting Apart

Talk to me please
Tell me where we stand
I can feel the tension
I just want to understand,
Are we okay?
Is there something on your mind?
You have to communicate
Then things will be fine.
The silence seems louder
Than any fight we've ever had before
Can you sit? Can we talk?
Why do you keep heading for the door?
We aren't the same, we don't talk anymore
Were drifting apart
I talk, but you constantly ignore
You can't expect things to work out
If there's nothing you want to talk about,
Trying to remain positive
And tell myself there's no one else
Because I know my worth
And this isn't what I deserve.

Communication is key
So why cant you talk to me?
No more dinner dates
We don't even stay up watching movies late
Its like you changed overnight
And I'm the only one fighting to make this right
If this isn't what you want
Then be a man and say so
But don't walk around on mute
When there's something I should know.

Please Don't Be Mad

Before you hear it from Drew
I need to tell you a thing or two
Please don't be mad
I don't want this secret to ruin what we had,
Before word gets around
We need to have a sit down
Don't look at me that way
Just listen to what I have to say,
He came over to the house
You were still out and about
I told him you were gone
And that he needed to get out
I wasn't expecting company
So I had on a robe and a thong
He leaned in for a kiss
I knew it was wrong
I went to turn away, things happened so fast
Before I knew it, his hands were cuffing my ass
Somehow we made it to the couch
Then he started eating me out
I got up and told him to leave

Though I wanted it, I felt like he violated me
Shit that sounds bad
I was caught up in the moment
You know you're my king
Its you that I've chosen,
I don't now what to do to make this up to you
I don't know if we can recover
Or will we just keep hurt8ig one another?
It kills me inside to see the pain in your eyes
But I wanted to be honest and not live with lies
I know that you hate me
I'm probably every bitch in the book
I feel your blood boiling
I see the rage in your looks
Can you please forgive me?
I don't want this to tear us apart
Please don't be mad
I truly love you from the bottom of my heart.

My Baby Boy

This little boy came into my life
6 pounds, 8 ounces cute as can be
I'm happy he's mine
I love him for eternity,
He brings me joy
He's my precious baby boy
At times when I want to give up
I look at him
And gain my strength back again
He gives ne this feeling
Like I'm the greatest person in the world
I'm not gonna lie, I wanted a baby girl
But having a son
Has changed my whole world
He's everything I ever wanted
He's my favorite kid
I walk into a room
And his world lights up
He adores me, and loves my presence
I just cant get enough of him
I love him so much

In ways I never knew I could
If I could experience child birth again
I definitely would,
The minute I leave the room
His eyes fill with tears,
"Don't cry baby boy, mommy's right here."
Being alone is one of his biggest fears
No matter where I go in life
Having him was my biggest achievement
God gave you to me for a reason
I have my little Kyng
One that I can call my own
This little boy is my everything
Joy to my life is what he brings
He teaches me how to be a better person
Inside and out
I live for my son
That's what motherhood is all about
I love my son with all of my heart
Jaedyce gave me a reason for life,
And I brand new fresh start.

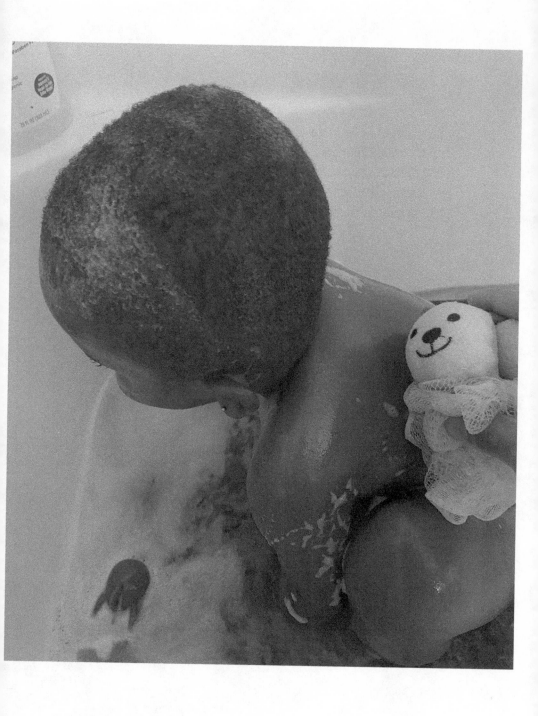

Are We Sisters?

I don't understand
Why you dislike me so much
No matter what I do
You're always there so cause a fuss,
Full blooded sisters
But you could never tell
We came out the same bomb
But on earth she treats me like hell,
You're the older sister
Im supposed to look up to you
But you envy me so much
And seek competition in everything I do,
Are we really sisters?
The shit has me puzzled
We'll never have a relationship
You've been nothing but trouble,
Everything is rivalry
You always try to top what I do,
I have a new car
So now you have a new car too?

Plans of buying a house til Covid came along
You took the class online
So you could buy your house first
And beat me to the finish line,
All I want is a sibling
That I can get along with
And talk to about anything
Instead I'm stuck with a bitch
Who always wants to jump in the boxing ring
We can never get along
For more than a week
You just love drama
And negativity is all you seek
Before I leave
One last thing is bothering me,
Hey there sister... why do you really hate me?

Watching Him Suffer

It paralyzed his mind,
And took over his body
Embarrassed as hell
To see his photos in the lobby,
Strung out.... I cant find him anywhere
I circle the blocks
At the liquor store
He stands there
Numb.. he doesn't even know what to say
He's hurting inside
Knowing that his baby girl sees him this way
Taking him to programs
Sitting in meetings
Holding his hand
He disappears for some weeks
My heart is heavy, I cant get any sleep,
Where is he? Is he okay?
Its not fair that his kids feel this way
Worried... I'm stressed
What if the drugs get the best?
Trying to convince him
To sober up and stay clean
Praying I'll wake up and this will all be a dream
He sits in the court, begging to be free
He's banned from the stores
His freedom now has a fee
I know it sounds harsh
But I left him in there
It's the only way he'll get help
Maybe he'll see that I care

This thing is on going
It just doesn't go away
The drugs keep coming back
His sobriety I pray,
He's the first man I've ever loved
He's my best friend
Yes I'm a daddy's girl
So I can't let the drugs win,
I need my hero back
I'm trying to remain strong
The drugs keep winning
What the fuck am I doing wrong?
I'm talking to a wall
I just cant get through to him
You have grandkids now
What do we tell them?
You're missing birthdays
Ours is just six days apart
I cant find you anywhere
This is breaking my heart,
I open my social media
There's memes everywhere
I zoom in close,
Is that my dad right there?
My soul is aching
God please tell me what I lack
Dear heroin,
Can I have my dad back?
-Dedicated

Kenneka Jenkins

I didn't know you I person
But this case has me hurting
19 years old
And just left in the cold,
Setup by your "friends"
Beaten, raped and sold
Your mom made profit
This world is so fuckin cold!
Fake videos,
Everyone was involved
The worlds not stupid
That wasn't her in those halls
Everything was staged
They went to two hotels
I hope all you fake bitches
Get your karma in hell,
The gangs stalked her very move
She was tortured for days
By three different dudes
They hid the fiitage
Amd altered the tapes,
Police, the hotel managers
All knew she was being raped
I listen to her EVP's
She just wants justice
A whole life taken
But everyone's scared to discuss it,
Surveillance hidden,
No one saw a thing

Her body was cold
As her fake friend stole her ring
Every week there's a new break
In the case
Videos being released,
But none shows how she ended up deceased
Ruled out as an accident
The feds wont get involved,
All the people want to see
Is this young girls case being solved
Its been a year
Ans he doesn't even have a tombstone
No flowers at her grave site
Her family knows that just isn't right,
More than fifty people
Played a part in her death
Just say what happened
So baby girl can rest,
They walk on eggshells
Afraid to speak the truth
Why don't you have a heart?
What if that was someone related to you?
Can someone please speak up
Who are you protecting?
Kenneka's soul is ready to rest
No one has the right to take a life away,
Just tell us how she got in that freezer
That's all you have to say.
-Dedicated

16 Hours

16 hours,
You have 16 hours to live
Call your moms phone
Say goodbye to your kid,
Save all your tears
You missed court so you dodged all the years
16 hours
You have 16 hours to live
Make a live video
Tell the world what you did,
And you're about to sew what you reap
16 hours
You have 16 hours to live,
Write a suicide note
Then come grab onto this rope,
Don't make me change my mind
Your life is on the line
16 hours,
You have 16 hours to live
Today you will learn
Not to photograph young kids
I ain't start your life
But everyone's waiting for it to end,
16 hours

You have 16 hours to live
Don't beg now
Because we won't forgive
Beyond disgusting
You're just at the parks lusting
In 16 hours
You'll regret what you did
Stole the innocence of a child,
Another traumatized kid.

Work

Stuck in this place
That they call work
Two hours into my shift
And my head starts to hurt,
I never know what I'm walking into
Which mood my clients are in
The world of mental health
Switches by the minute
They can't control the voices
Some think they see faces
Black, Puerto Rican, Italian,
All different ages and races
They run into the wall at full speed
Not even caring that they're bleeding
One likes little children
Not realizing his age
People see this client and start to fill with rage
A girl abused by her dad
The voices and a baby
Is all she ever had,
They have no family
No one comes to visit them
Its sad, they're abandoned

Left to the system
Everyday at work it's a constant struggle
They say leave your feelings at the clock
But to most of my clients, the staff is all they got,
Tomorrow's a new day
Their personalities will change
Today they're your friend
Tomorrow that'll all end,
So when I get home
I'll pour a double shot
Don't judge me
The booze are all that I've got
To escape the madness
From witnessing so much pain and sadness
To numb it all and block out the hurt
Time to clock in, and get back to work.

Focus (3:37am)

Have you ever sat in the room full of people
Staring at the wall
Everyone's talking,
But conversations... you cant recall
You get up and walk to the bathroom
Tears streaming down your face,
"Shake it off, focus"
You wash up so there's no trace
Everything I look at reminds me of us
Years down the drain
Coping with knowing, things will never be the same
My boss is in the room
So I try to act sane,
They know somethings up
They're calling out my named
I cant look up, the tears will fall
I have to get it together,
Take a walk down the hall
Images replay in my head
23 hours out of the day
I wish I were dead
"Drink some water, you've got to relax"
Avoid the questions
If they start to ask
I just want to scream!

Crazy thoughts fill my mind
"Why the fuck am I here?"
I cant fight the tears,
What did I do

To make him fall out of love with me?
I grab my keys,
"I have to leave."
I sit in the car
The tears just don't stop,
I know this isn't right,
Emotions I try to fight
I have to be strong,
Pick the baby up from school,
He'll ask how was work...
I'll play it off and keep cool
We go to the park,
My mind still isn't there
Every song on the radio
Makes me wish he was here
You have to shake it off,
You have to be strong,
Because the drug you loved
So thorough and true
Has no feelings... back for you.

Was I Ever Enough?

I never thought
I was capable of loving
A man so much my heart aches
At the image of you,
Not once did I think
That it would hurt me this much
I'm a libra so I love hard
There is no giving up
There's no such thing as breaks
We'll talk until we make-up
You wanted the easy way out
Which is leaving me with doubts
Why waste seven years?
Why not try to work it out?
If I go to bat for our love
Why are you just standing there?
I'm focused on us
But your mind seems to be elsewhere
I beat myself up constantly
Was I ever enough?
Why aren't you saying anything?
What are you thinking of?
Trying to figure out
Where we could have went wrong
When did we even drift away

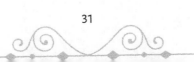

Has it been this long?
My heart is begging for closure
You have to say something
Even if I know its bullshit
Give me something to run with,
I stayed in shape,
I cooked and cleaned
Even satisfied you sexually
So what did I do
To make you look the other way?
Stop with the silent treatment
I know you have something to say,
He grabbed my hand softly
And said its not what it seems,
"You're my best friend, my lover,
You are the woman of my dreams."
It's not you, it's me
Sorry baby...
But I play for the other team.

Emotions

All I see is red,
Anger and hurt fill my heart
I can't control the tears
I can't get back 7 wasted years,
Competing with females
I see in your DM
Why keep fuckin with me
When you've always wanted them?
We've joined a game
Of who can hurt who the most,
I throw the towel in!
This shit hurts, you win!
I can't imagine you happy with someone else
That wasn't the plan
When we decided to have little man,
It hurts when I hear your name
Reality sets in,
I know things won't be the same
I try to be tough
I numb the pain
But when the drugs wear off
My heart still hurts the same
Messages from four years ago to last week
Embedded in my head
If it wasn't for our son
I would've been faked my own death
"You're not supposed to love

A person this much"
The pain just doesn't ease
Love is a very dangerous disease
I block your number
Thinking it would help
But I keep reaching out
I can't help myself,
When were you going to tell me
That I was never enough?
My heart keeps racing
I don't know if this is a panic attack
I don't know how you got me like that!
The image of you,
Giving them your touch
Hurts me to my core,
Makes me wish I didn't love you anymore,
I really wish I didn't love you this way,
God, please help me...
What the fuck do I say?
The devil has won
But this game was not even fun
I want my soul back,
You can have my heart,
Cause when I gave it to you
It was broken from the start.

Why? (4:27am)

Up crying and stressing
You're probably in her bed being messy,
I thought I was protecting my heart
But love had me blinded from the start
Worse than post-partum
Depression has kicked in
Emotions run high,
Drinking has become my best friend
I just needed closure, so I can move on
My heart will never be whole
I understand what we once had is now gone
I just want to know
If you ever truly loved me?
I can't think of a time
That I went through your phone
And didn't find something that hurt me
I thought we were repairing our friendship
Building a foundation for our son,
We had future goals on becoming a unit as one!
Days went by and you wouldn't check on us,
Now... I see why
You said there were no others
Why did you have to lie?
Why would you jeopardize
Our son having a stable home

Were they worth it?
Why did you disrespect the throne?
You could have saved me
A lot of heartache
If you were honest back then,
Who knows where we could have been
Don't reply, I'm not going to check
My blocked messages
My heart is just heavy
So I'm using my words to express me
Our son is doing fine,
I have to protect his heart and mine
He thinks you're coming home
Poor kid, he didn't ask for any of this!
All I can do is distract his mind and mine
Games, parks, shopping, making sure he doesn't sleep alone
Anything to avoid him asking
When's daddy coming home
I just have one last question
Then I'll leave you alone,
Did you ever really want a family?
Or want to marry me?
I just need to know
So I can set my heart free.

I Put A Band-Aid On It

I put a band-id on it,
I don't want it to bleed
I don't want to talk about it
Don't ask what he meant to me,
I put a band-aid on it
When they see our son
They stop to speak
Please don't ask,
I dot want to relive the past
I put a band-aid on it,
I shame myself everyday
What have I done
To ever be treated this way?
I put a band-aid on it
My first real heart break
Lesson learned I guess,
My heart failed the best
I put a band-aid on it
Just leave it there!
I don't need to be reminded
Every time I change my hair,
Or I get a new tattoo
Every chapter of my life
I change my appearance
Avoid living with strife,
I just want to be happy
But that just isn't possible

Somethings just aren't meant to be a success,
I can't seem to reach
I picked up an extra job
But working eighty hours a week is killing me
Not only that, but our son
I barely get to see
He acts out because he needs his mom and dad
My son and my tears
Are all I have left
My heart constantly hurts,
There's no off switch
Who said this was fair?
One sided love is a bitch,
I put a band-aid on it
I don't want it to bleed
My heart breaks again
When they ask, "how have you been?"
I put a band-aid on it,
"How is Raheem?"
I just sit there in sorrow,
Emotional... and bleed.

Grieve (6:24am)

Do a wellness check,
"She's not picking up!"
It's not like her
To miss this much work,
"Call her cell."
Straight to voicemail,
"Does anyone have a key?"
"You gotta check with Fe."
Behind the door
Lies a cold body on the floor
She couldn't fake being alright anymore
A white piece of paper lies near a toy dinosaur....

"To my Kyng,
Know that mommy loves you dearly
Always be my big boy that I taught you to be,
You're one of a kind and made out of love
A word so strong, so cruel when misused
You have a host of family and loved ones
Who will be there for you,
You'll never go without
I left everything to you!
Never let anyone take advantage of my little man
I raised you to be a soldier
Anything you want to do, you can!
You're too young to understand

What I was going through,
But deep down in spirit with you!
Don't cry, I want you to be happy
We've had a lot of fun,
Just you and I.
"Mommy play my song!"
I can just hear your precious laugh,
Your personality will get you far
You light up a room!
I know it'll be tough,
But accept your new mom,
Be kind to her and pray to me at night
I've got to go son,
I love you dearly!
Tell your dad I can't forgive him,
Now my soul is forever empty."

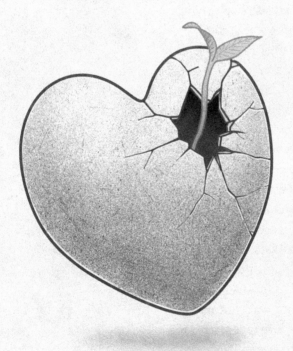

Control

It's Friday night
And he's working late again
The ladies want to go out,
"I don't know, t's up to him."
They look at me strange
And tell me I've changed
But they don't know what I go through
When I disobey you,
I'm not allowed to lock my phone,
I can't go outside alone,
People always judge us
Not knowing it's hard for you to trust
You just want me to yourself
I can't have eyes for anyone else
Most calls are on speaker
If not he'll fucking beat her,
He gets home from work at 11:53
Dinner has to be done, or he'll punish me
I thought it was cute at first
Until the love taps started to hurt
I knew he was serious
When he gave me a curfew
I called my mom and told her
What I was going through

"J'Naye what are you letting him do to you?"
Everyone told me to leave
But that just can't be
He does a lot for me
And I haven't even told him
That we're expecting a baby,
He said when the day comes
And I'm pregnant with his seed
I'll want to thank him
For everything he's taught me
I'll be ready for marriage
And I might be the one
I was off for a few days,
Light headed, my mind was in a daze
I forgot to do his laundry
So Monday he back slapped me
He apologized instantly,
I'm pretty sure this isn't how love is supposed to be
The door bell rang, it was my friend
She wanted to come in,
I told her to hold on one second,
"I have to check with him"
She grabs my wrist softly,
Flashbacks made me flinch,

"Sis, what has he done to you?"
"Nothing, I'm fine"
"When did he start the abuse?"
He comes out the room to see who I'm talking to
"You can go, you're not welcomed here"
I try to stand tall and fight back the tears
"It's over, I'm leaving, I can't live like this"
I've suffered too long
This isn't where I belong
He cocks his fist back
He's ready to swing
My friend pulls out a gun
The shots make my ears ring,
"What have you done?!"
"Where did you even get that from?"
"I had to save you,
I had to save the abuse, you're my best friend
I couldn't let him keep hurting you."
Sad and in shock
Trying not to be mad,
I ended the suffering
But my kid will never meet their dad.

Catfished

Screenshot a thirsty picture
She has to be cute,
He has to be interested in her
Then make your first move,
Slide in his DMs
You have to make the conversation deep
Don't sound like yourself
And don't come off as a creep
Flirt with him,
We have to wheel him in
Get him right where I want him
Then the fun begins,
I know he wont resist
He's addicted to the internet
Five bucks says he'll respond
Come on lets make a bet,
Weeks pass, yes we still speak
He's willing to risk his own family
Dumb ass she's really me!
He's telling her things
That I've heard before
She's his favorite girl,
The one that he truly adores
He wants to re-locate
He wants to finally move
Come on guy... are you really this dumb of a dude?
You're in love with a stranger

Just some words on a screen
I should tell him it was me
I should stop before this gets messy
Instead I'll cause a fight
And let him know
That his actions weren't right
I'll call him a cheater
And tell him to go be with her
He'll give me this look,
With innocence on his face
But I've read all the texts
Such a fucking disgrace,
He's done this before
But this time it hits home
He's shown me he's a dog
He just wants to roam
I'll have an attitude
Walk by him without saying a word
I'll act like he's invisible
Not even caring that it'll hurt
Can guys be that stupid?
Just look at him
He makes me want to lose it!
Trying to hold it together
I have to be strong
I did it so he'll let me go,
Now we both can finally move on.

Wadi (Dedicated)

Fresh into senior year
No one knew what I was struggling through
Dodging social workers
My only sanity was with you,
I created another personality while we were together
I was happy, free, laughed uncontrollably
You showed me things that girls my age shouldn't see
Did I mind?
Not at all, because I loved your company
I found a true friend in you, a lover and escape route
I could be myself, vent and not get judged
You taught me to be strong
And showed me what the streets were all about
You were older so we often clashed
I was young but mature
You understood things that I often endured
We stopped talking after I graduated
I guess we just drifted apart
No matter what time it was
You would check on me and remind me that I still held had your heart
Im used to receiving a call from you
When I visit my aunt in Hartford
But after three visits without a word
I had to reach out and make sure you were good
I called your phone and kept getting voicemail
I googled your name hoping to see a social media page
My heart sank and I could not breathe
I couldn't believe my eyes or what they were showing me

It just couldn't be, not Wadi's obituary
I called your grandmother but not knowing what to say
Just tell me this isn't true, tell me he's okay
"Sweetheart, I lost your number... the funeral was the other day"
My emotions are raging, I've never felt this way before
I make my way to Bloomfield
Pedal to the floor
She gave me a hat of yours, a pin with your face on it
Your friend stopped by to share the news
I just don't understand, you were such a great dude
A car accident, two blocks from your house
The cops were being racist and wouldn't let anyone help you out
Dead at the scene, I couldn't believe what I was reading
I went to the cemetery to speak with you
And let you understand that I will always appreciate you
I will always have love for you, remember you and the fun times
we had
I just felt so horrible, I felt so bad
I lost my best friend and the only man that I could depend
I want you to rest easy and keep me close to your heart
Just know that I love you and I hate that were apart
I know you're my guardian angel,
I can feel it in my soul
Sometimes I don't know how I make it home safe intoxicated
Then I think of you, you always told me I would make it
I love you dearly and it hurts that I couldn't say goodbye
"So Wavy" on your Max,
Forever... You and I.
Dedicated to Horace Richards Jr.

Loners Block

Sometimes I sit and think
Maybe its not them, maybe it's me
Running from the truth
When all I need is to face reality,
I have a special gift
Of attracting the perfect men
But then something rubs me the wrong way
And I become distant that same day,
I start to catch feelings
Get attached, then go missing,
Its like something stops me in my tracks
And makes me hold my guard back,
I don't know how to submit
I'm broke, I can finally admit
But a good woman indeed
I just need the right man to be patient with me,
I cook, I clean, iron and do laundry
Faithful and a family woman
I just need security
So my mind and body can relax within,
Some men see that as a sign of weakness
But that's not the case

There's just some things that I have to face,
All I'm used to is being hurt
So I don't know exactly how this love thing works
I know I'm supposed to give it my all
And not bring old problems into a new relationship
But when I see certain signs
I have to avoid certain shit,
To protect my heart
And not waste my time
Not get wrapped up in a fairytale
Or be stupid and believe you're only mine,
But then again that's me, pushing you away
Wanting you to be closer
But not knowing how to ask you to stay
I want this to work
And I want us to last
I'm trying I am,
I'm just scarred from my past.

Lost Trust

You haven't done anything
To make me feel this way
I was scorned from my past
A flaw I must say
I'm so used to being hurt
And especially lied to
I hear what you say
But it seems too good to be true
You could tell me it's raining
And I'll have to double check
I know I have to trust
I just haven't crossed that bridge yet
Your job doesn't help any of my insecurities
Your surrounded by girls
The night life is a whole different world
You deserve a fair shot
I want to give "us" all that I got
I just can't bare another heartbreak
So I love from a distance
The moment I think your lying
I become ghost in an instant
I'm sorry you walked into this
I should have told you from the start
You deserve better
At least a fair chance at winning my heart
We talk all the time

We're glued to the phone
But that's not enough
We have to separate homes
I want to open up
And completely let you in
I'm trying, I promise
Just don't throw the towel in
Please be patient with me
While I learn to trust again
I'm sorry I didn't tell you all this in the beginning
I want to give you my all
And not look stupid in the end
I just need some more time
I promise it'll be worth the win
Just be honest, no little white lies
Stand out from the rest
Show me you aren't like the other guys
Get your mind off the prize
Get to know me inside and out
Be transparent so I wont have any doubts
Show me you're worthy of my heart and trust
Because getting married is an ultimate must
I'm going to trust you
So please give me time
My heart will be yours
And forever you'll be mine.

Work Wife

I guess your not happy at home
Or you wanna be a dirty dick nigga
And start to roam
I see the way she looks at you
Then you grab your phone,
You must think I'm dumb
I can see the chemistry,
Have you slept with her?
Have you shared intimacy?
Would I be wrong if I told you
That you had to let her go?
Its 8am and you got me
Thinking about drinking liquor
Three times this week
I've tried to surprise you with lunch
The secretary says sorry
You guys just left for brunch,
Unscheduled meetings,
now you're taking late night conference calls
you're testing my gangsta
I'll burn down your office

Then you'll say that I'm crazy
No nigga, your trippin
I know what I see
Your ass is just slippin
You can pack your stuff
Since you just can't get enough
You didn't even say happy birthday today
I swear you hurt me in the worst ways,
I saw your car parked where her loft is,
Don't worry nigga
I'll leave all your shit at the corporate office.

Dedicated

This man walked into my life
And stole my heart without permission
I didn't even get mad
Because he's everything I've been missing
He gives me butterflies
He's not like other guys
He's passionate when he speaks
I can see it in his eyes
His smile lights up my day
I've never had a guy
Make me feel this way
He accepts my for who I am,
My past, he understands
Though he's miles away
I still feel like he's near me everyday
I want him closer so we can expand our family
Make memories and build a legacy,
He checks on me daily
And always treats me like a lady
He's become my best friend
Damn, where has this man been
I feel like I'm in high school
Whenever I'm near him
I can't stop blushing or smiling
And he showers me with attention
I wake up and thank God
For placing such a wonderful man in my path,
He's given me hope again
So I'll make sure that we last.

Silence

Young and abused
I was too young to be misused
So ashamed and afraid
My heart filled with rage
I don't know who to tell
I just wish I'd go to hell
Why was I home alone?
Why were my parents so trusting
Men coming in and out our home
Your daughters they were lusting
I just hit my teens
Shit what does this mean?
I'm supposed to choose
When to lose my virginity
You still show your face
And you're not ashamed
I opened up and told my family
Hoping they would help ease the pain
My sister said get over it
And gave her son your name
I'm constantly reminded of what I've been through
I always see his face when I look at my nephew
Family cookouts... who the fuck invited you?
No one took me serious

That's why I don't mention what I've been through
He damaged me as a child
That's why I isolated for awhile
Growing up not trusting men
Because I'm afraid to get hurt again
No on knows what its like
To have your rapist over for dinner
Everyone accepts him
Because he had a kid with your sister
Tuning everyone out
They don't give a fuck anyway
I'll sit in silence
And just wait for judgement day.

Insecure

You want me to trust you
And put my guard down
Don't second guess your actions
And believe you aren't messing around,
You want a clean slate
And for me to open up
You want to break down walls
And completely remove the gate
Not get suspicious
Even when you come home late,
You want me to be confident in our relationship
Baby I cant do that
But certain thigs I don't deal with
I should have came with a warning
Or caution sticker
So you'd know what you're getting into
Instead of my insecurities shocking you
You're right, I shouldn't judge you
Based on my past
But how can I be certain
You're nothing like the last?
Guys will sweet talk you

They all say the same thing
Just a different voice
But the game remains the same
The lies get better
Shit, some even written love letters
Introduce you to mom just after two dates
Swear you're the one and only,
And you're their soulmate
You want me to trust you
You promise you're not the same,
"Not all men lie"
You must think I'm insane
I guess you can say I'm damaged
I'll thank my ex for that,
Here... take your phone,
Text those three girls back.

Kidnapped

It's dark in here,
Wait why are we moving?
Where are we going?
What do you think you're doing?
Mom said lock the door
Then she went into the store
I said I'll be alright
But unexpectedly hit in the head
All I see is lights
In the back of moms truck
Two men are driving, I should've listened,
"What the fuck?"
I kick the backseat
And ask what do they want
He looks at me with rage,
Speeds up and the horn he starts to honk
I know that time is ticking
And I have to act fast
I don't know where we're going or how long it'll last
I try to reach for my phone
But out the window its thrown
Don't worry, don't panic

Mom will get me back home,
I start to smell a scent
One that I've smelled before
It lingers in the car
Next, I hear the car door
"This wasn't the plan"
Says the voice of a familiar man
"Just keep your voice down"
You don't understand
We're moving again
Damn I should have ran
My eyes are being covered
All I see is shadows
"Are you going to hurt me?
I just want to know,
My mom has money
If that's what you're after."
"Just shut up little girl
That doesn't even matter
I recognize the fragrance
The shape od his head too

My lips start to tremble,
"Dad is that you?"
The car get quiet
He excels on the gas,
"I'm sorry for this, it'll be over fast"
We stopped again, but this time is different
Its taking very long
Butterflies fill my stomach
Tell me somethings wrong
The door closes,
An unfamiliar voice says to me,
"Sorry honey, now you belong to me"
Money changes people,
Makes them evil you see?
At age 14 I'm an old mans property
What the fuck is love
When you're kidnapped
And sold by you own daddy?

Chasing Bad Boys

Your mom would be so happy
The day you bring her home
She's perfect, sweet and loyal
You even have the code to her phone,
She loves hard and always thinks of you
though her friends warned her not to
the chemistry can't be broken
negativity is always spoken
she's such a good girl
who the hell would've ever knew
the ideal perfect couple
even strangers envy you
"What makes her want a bad boy?
Her father won't approve."
He puts a glow on her
So the rumors he'll disprove
Whenever they're together
No one else matters
He's charming and sweet
So appearances never flatter,
He's not in the streets
But he always wears red,
He's not a D-Boy

No one's out for his head
He's been around the block
So of course people judge
But who are they to discriminate
The type of person I should love?
He makes me happy
A happy that I've never been
Not only is he my man
But he's also my best friend
It's not up to us to convince you
Why good girls chase bad boys
He's hood but he's sweet
He also brings me joy
So please don't judge us
Because I'm wearing heels
And he has timberlands on,
That's the problem with this generation
They always find something wrong
I love him to the moon and back,
We just wish you guys would accept that!

My Sister

Four sisters, four brother
Only half of us have the same mother
But you and I share a bond
That can never be broken
I tell everyone you're my favorite
They think I be joking
We became very close
When I needed my family the most
After my car wreck
You were all hands on deck,
I couldn't describe the pain I was feeling
But you helped me a lot
Especially when my body was healing,
I didn't think that you would stay this long
I mean I love your company
Don't get me wrong!
Usually you're with the other sister
You know... the enemy
I'm not gonna lie, that used to get to me
You've become my best friend
We talk about almost everything
You've been there through my break-ups
You've witnessed all my pain
You've seen me at my highest
You've also seen me when I was low
I appreciate you so much

In ways you'll never know,
Your nephew adores you
You're his best friend too
You're such a great sister
We both love you!
From my stylist to movie date,
I love our quality time
There's not enough to share
So tell Raekwon you're mine!
Eight siblings, one tattoo
They all hate our relationship
Your twin does too
I just want to say
I've watched you blossom everyday
You're such a lovable person
Sometimes too caring
But look how far we made it
Without a single parent
You're the daughter I always wanted
The best friend I tried to seek
Just remember I'm always here
If there's anything you'll ever need
I'll climb a thousand mountains
And swim a thousand seas,
Anything to be there for you
Because you were there for me.

-Dedicated to Felicia

Mind Fuck

The room crowds with people
But I only see you there
We lock eyes for a second
I smell your cologne in the air,
You walk over to me
And undress me with your eyes
You softly kiss my neck
Your hand is on my thighs
Your tongue traces my ear
You use your hand to move my hair,
I feel my panties getting wet
And we haven't even done anything yet
I feel your bulge
So chocolate and fat
You bite your lip
I know you like that,
My tongue licking every vein
And swallowing every inch
You whisper in my ear,
"daddy's freaky little bitch"
You bend me over,
Still kissing on my neck

Fighting the temptation
I know you want to have sex
You rub your hand down my back
Until you have a handful of ass
I'm starting to cave in
I don't know how long I can last
I open my legs just a little
So you can feel the middle
You moan, "damn baby" in my ear
I know you've never had
Good pussy like that in years,
You rub the tip of you dick
All through my juices
I'm trying not to cave in
But you know what you're doing
You're rubbing my nipples
I think I'm about to cum
This freaky ass nigga,
Look what you've done
The music gets loud
Standing out In the crowd
My panties are soaked

"this is a fucking joke"
Tall, chocolate, bearded and fine
Standing in the middle of the venue
I cannot believe
I just mind fucked the shit out of you!

Temptation

We're in the hotel
Drunk off the Cîroc
I keep holding back
But it' taking everything I got
In the middle of conversations
We just lock eyes
Your lips met mine
As you caressed my thighs
"Baby I want you!"
I told you to behave
We sit back down
And we resume the game
I've held back for seven months
But you have me so turned on
There's something about your lips
That has me so far gone
Before I knew it
We were kissing in bed
Your face drops down
And you start to give me head
Little do you know
Your kisses are making me wet
I need your lips up here

You haven't seen anything yet
Your lips make their way to my nipples
You know I'm about to cum
I feel every inch pressed against me
You tell me not to run,
Then you slide your monster in me
Pussy is gripping every inch
It fits so perfect, I swear the wait was worth it
Damn you're turning me on
Back to back strokes
Your juicy dick is so long
You're making me scream
Your dick is in my stomach
And my pussy starts to cream
You got me screaming "daddy"
I know the neighbors are mad at me
Biting the pillow
That shit was no help
You planned this perfectly,
Wouldn't wait to get me to yourself
Your back shots are insane I'm still moaning your name
We were supposed to behave
And just play a card game
You tell me you love me

Then mark me as your territory
I feel your warm cum fill up my insides
But baby that's a waste
I told you that I wanted to taste
We had no regrets,
That was the best part
We're madly in love, claiming each other's heart
We resume the game
With the same result
You know you are not slick
This is all your fault
Your dick is getting harder
So I sit on your lap
I wake up in the morning
Damn baby... did we really do that?

Co-Parenting

I know you're here to see our son
And this visit isn't about me
But seeing your face again
Brings back so many memories,
The words that I tried to heal
Begins to bleeds again
All the pain comes back
It's like I just can't win
We have an understanding
To focus on co-parenting
But you become absent
When you start talking to someone
It boils my blood
When you put bitches before your son
You tell me I'm crazy,
I'm seeing things wrong
But I believed your lies
For six years too long
You've created this woman
Whom you cannot stand
You broke a woman
Who would do anything for her man
I loved you so much

That even when you hurt me
I still tried to understand
Each visit with our son
Hurts a little bit more
Taking phone calls outside
I overheard you talking to whores
I know we just co-parent
But why did we waste six years?
So many sleepless nights
My pillow was soaked from the tears
Video chats get unanswered
Our son reaches out to you
You're active on Facebook though,
This is the stupid shit that you do
We can never be together
The trust is dead and gone
I just want to get closure
So my heart can move on
I need you to tell me
Why you left without a word
And don't shut me out
My voice needs to be heard
I need to release these feelings

My heart is holding onto
I need to somehow learn
How to get over you
I know we're just co-parenting
But thins were left unsaid
Feelings are still there
Somedays I can't get you out of my head
He's coming to see our son,
This visit isn't about me
Hide all emotions,
Let the relationship be history...

I Will Hold
Your Little Hand
But You Will
Hold My
Heart

Lost Child

She's alone and misused
She stays to herself
And not many people know
That she's been abused,
She attracts the wrong men
Anything for attention
She's not a fast ass
She just wants love and affection,
In and out of foster homes
Surrounded by do many people
But she still feels alone
Battling depression
But you saw her wrist
The trail marks they would show,
She's quiet and high maintenance
That's envy in their eyes,
She just wants to fit in
Feel normal for a change,
Make a friend or two
And stop living so estranged,
In high school she started drinking
She changed over the years
It's her way of soothing

Because alcohol taste better than tears,
Her and her mother didn't speak
No relationship at all
Her dads in jail
And he doesn't even call,
She starts online dating
Searching for companionship
Everyone judges her
All she wants is a relationship,
Trying to finish high school
Hiding under the radar
Missing open house
So people won't question where her parents are
Hiding it all
She stands tall and smiles
So before you judge her
Just sit and talk for a while.

Numb

She tried to be perfect
And show him she's worth it
She begged for a cjancve
For a shot at romance,
He led her to believe
She was everything he needs
Until she finds out one day
She was only being deceived
He needed a place to lay his head
So the lies she was fed,
Until he comes home
To find her almost dead
Tears in her eyes
They're blood shot red
Benadryl on the floor
She didn't want to live anymore
She consumed more than what was caused for
Her body feels numb
She's unaware of what she's done
Medics rush there
Her stomach gets pumped with air

Tring to save her life
He prays he can make this right
So sedated, she doesn't feel
So high, all of this seems unreal
"I never meant to hurt you"
He begins to pray,
"You're my earth, my moon,
Baby please pull through"
Her eyes open, she's surprised that he's still there
"All I really wanted was for you to care"
She grabs his hand
And squeezes it tight
He drops on one knee
And promises to change that night
She agrees to be his wife
If he makes things right,
Together forever,
For the rest of their lives.

Social Worker

The red car pulls up
I already know what that means
Their last words are always,
"It's not what it seems."
Everyday I'm alive
Feels like a bad dream
I don't understand
Why nobody wants me,
I sit at the office
While my social worker finds me a new home
I'm always with so many people
But yet, I feel so alone
The system doesn't care
They'll throw you anywhere
I've lived with rapist, roaches and rats
Molested at 13, yep... all that
I'm not even a bad kid
I'm not even in the system for something that I did!
My mom got in a car wreck
She's been in a coma every since
The system snatched me up
Now everything is tense
I have no family here
So I needed alternative care,

My worker is ready to go
This means I have a new home
I share a room with others
But I'm still alone
Two days later, the red car pulls up
I already know the routine
There's just no right fit for me
I just want to go home
Or to visit my mother,
The system is cruel
God when will she recover?
Trying not to be a statistic
This is draining me
I just want to be a normal kid,
For once, please?
I'll hold on a little longer
For my mom, I'll be stronger
Can someone just take me in
And keep me for a week
Tired of living out of trash bags
I'm not a bad kid, give me a chance
You'll see!

Who Sent you?

I often ask myself,
"How the hell did I get so lucky?"
"Who sent you to me?
How did they know where I'd be?"
You make ne a different kind of happy
One that I've never seen
It's like you're everything I dreamed of
Dipped in chocolate and personalized for me,
I thought I was crazy
Because I can't get you off my mind
I feel so obsessed,
Because I miss you all the time
Even when you're asleep
Or when you're at work,
I think about you all day,
I think about you so much
You know what I'm thinking without me saying a word
You know how to make me smile
With all of your charm and flirts
I daydream about you so much
I'm afraid my head will start to hurt,
You accept all of my flaws
And help me with my insecurities
We talk for hours on the phone
You show me that you're really here for me
When I've had a long day

You're the only one I want to run to
I know that you'll be supportive
In any situation I'm going through
You show me that you care
When I start to doubt your interest
When I start to pull away,
You grab me closer
And assure me you're here to stay
The perfect day off
Consists of me laying in your arms
Because when I'm with you
I feel safe and protected from harm
The way you hold me when I'm asleep,
I could lay there forever
I finally have my prince charming
I'm so happy we're together,
I've always longed for a man like you
Attentive and caring,
Even when I become insecure
You prove to me I'm not sharing,
My love for you grows
Stronger and deeper each day
I don't know who sent you
But I hope you're here to stay
You're my biggest blessing this year

And the only man
That hasn't brought my eyes to tears
I love you and I appreciate you
Including everything you do
I'm glad I found my best friend
And a soulmate in you,
I love you more than
I could ever show
Patiently waiting to say, "I love you"
And watch our future grow,
You have my heart
Please handle it with care
If ever you shall need something
Please tell me, I'll be there
I don't know who sent you
But I'm happy you've arrived
I thank God for sending me
The man of my life!

Missing You Different

I haven't seen you in a week
This feelings different now,
I miss you immensely
You cologne fills the air
I inhale your scent and bite my lip
Imagining you kissing me and pulling my hair
I've been longing for your touch
Just to be close to you
I feel the volcanos irrupt,
I want you to pull me close
And show me how much you miss me
Shower me with love
And caress me passionately,
Let your fingers roam every inch of my body
I don't want it to be brief
I want all of that chocolate inside me,
Lets fulfill all of your fantasies
Let me show you what you mean to me
We lock eyes as we kiss softly
My pussy throbbing for you
Baby just take all of me,
A laugh and giggle here and there,
"Stop being so bad"

We just can't help it
I want you near, we finally cave in
We're going round for round
The neighbors hear every sound
There's juices everywhere
Loud moans as you pull on my hair
You slowly stroke the start to pound
The headboard is squeaking
My g-spot you just found,
My back is arched
You make me squirt everywhere
You start kissing
And licking it up without a care,
"Daddy I miss you"
I know that shit turs you on,
A hour later
We're still fucking to the same song
Your strokes are getting deeper
Your fucking me like I did something wrong
Your pip is insane
So thick and so long,
"Daddy let me taste it"
I think I need a break

My legs are trembling and my body aches
The bed is drenched, wetter than a lake
You get into a rhythm
That's how I know you're ready
You let off your rounds
Your loads are so heavy,
We stare into each others eyes
And admire what we just did
Sex so passionate and intense
I know I'll be having you r kid,
You tell me you love me
And I love you too,
It's been a long week
I just wanted to show you
How much I missed you.

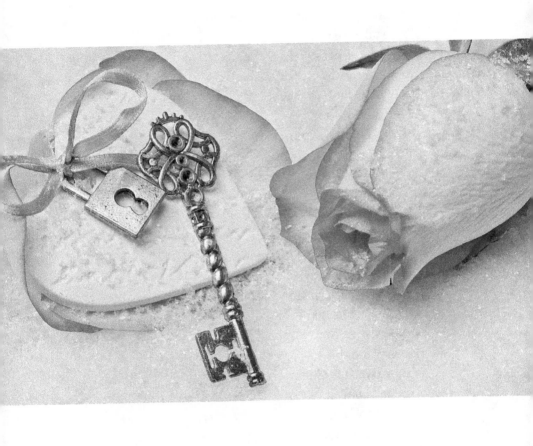

Becoming An Alcoholic

Its been a long day
Exhausting and tiring, but I know what I need
Just to take the pain away,
I'll stop at the packy
They know me by my first name
Don't judge me and call me,
Or call me an alchy,
Somedays its only one or two
Other days I can't function without the booze
It seems like my escape route
Or the only listening ear
When my head is filled with doubts,
At night when I cant sleep,
Its always there to comfort me
Right on the floor, outside of the pantry
It gives me confidence and numbs my horrible thoughts
Is this really a drug?
Or a legal medicine I just brought?
Don't tell me I have a problem
Because you don't know my pain,
You don't understand
That alcohol keeps me sane,
My mind is still racing after 3 shots,
I'll open some champagne

To blur out the thoughts
Everything is blurry,
I'm getting tired now
My mind is finally quiet,
Not a single sound
I wake up and feel like shit
My hair all over the place
I have to clean up
So I don't go into work looking like a disgrace,
My phone is filled with hate mail
And calls that I don't remember making
I still feel a buzz
My hands are still shaking,
I'm working on getting sober,
I long for a day
That I don't have a hangover,
I'll go to the package store again after work
Don't shake your head,
It stops all the hurt
Just let me have my booze
And leave me in peace,
Becoming an alcoholic...
Please don't judge me.

Miscarriage

It seems like an ordinary day
Until you get up to use the bathroom
And suddenly drop to you knees to pray,
All I see is red,
But I don't understand
I ate healthy, worked out
This pregnancy was planned!
My heart hurts so much
It feels heavy, and sharp
Like its waiting to burst,
All I do is cry while ruining the bathroom rug
God please tell me this isn't true
My prays don't seem to reach up above,
How do I tell my husband?
I cant call him at work
But he'll hate me for not calling
No on knows how bad this hurts,
I didn't get to meet you
But I dreamed of your face
We were so happy and anxious
We wanted to name you Chase,
Beating myself up,
I don't know what I could have done wrong
I call my doctor up
She just tells me to be strong
I'm sitting in a puddle of red
Devastated and torn

Wishing to God I was dead,
Do you know what its like
To have a bond with someone you haven't locked eyes with?
To see a face on the screen
For nine months you wait to meet,
Then without warning
All of that is taken away
I don't know wat to do
This is one fucked up day,
Someone please help me
I've never been through this
I lost a child while asleep
What did I miss?
Home alone and confused
Hurt like I've never hurt before
Broken in ways
That I wasn't prepared for,
I love you little baby
Indeed me and daddy do
Praying for understanding
Or for the lord to take me too.

Black Lives Matter

I turn on the news
It's the same shit everyday
A black man fighting for his life
The cops neglecting his rights,
Racist men dressed in blue
They carry a gun
So they think they have the rights to abuse,
Scared to pullover
When you see the flights lights
You never know nowadays if that will be
Your last night alive
Scared to send our kids to school
Quebec officers use too much force
What's it going to take for
The laws to be enforced,
"Hands up don't shoot"
They aim anyway,
Anything to make another black family
Suffer in dismay,
"Get your knee off my neck so I can breathe"
Nothing gets through to the white man
They kill us for the fun of it
Because Trump makes them feel like they can,
Watching a man's life
Be taken in broad daylight
Causes feud and anger

Towards everyone white,
"Justice for Breonna Taylor"
She was so young and innocent
No arrest have been made,
No one's taking accountability for what they did,
This world is cruel, yet very corrupt
African American's walk on eggshells
Half of the works remains shook,
Let's not forget what happened to Rayshard Brooks,
So many young lives have been taken away,
"No justice, no peace"
Please put the guns down
Use your voices and speak!
Black lives matter
I'll scream it til' I'm blue in the face
Justice for every innocent life taken
Please get closure for every case.

Covid-19

A normal day suddenly turns fatal
We were grieving from the loss of
The famous Koby Bryant
We didn't pay attention to the virus standing by us,
No one took it serious and others over panicked
Shelves were empty
Everyone was running around frantic,
We're told to isolate, grab a mask and keep your distance
Our lives changed quick,
Jobs and schools closed in an instance
Forced to stay at home
A test of everyone's strength
God forbid you're being abused
Because there's only virtual help,
No place you can run to,
The slightest headache or stuffy nose
People are looking at you funny,
Like, "that's not just a cold"
Bodies carried out and buried in random parks
Millions are dying, I gotta turn off the news
It gets worse everyday
I only leave the house to get booze,
Young teens still throwing parties
Please stop the spread,
They don't take Covid serious

Until someone they love is now dead,
Social distance, I never thought
I'd have a virtual doctor's appointment
I can't even see my therapist
Or complete half of the things on my daily to-do list,
All gatherings have been cancelled,
Funerals, weddings and first birthdays
We have never seen a virus this bad
It makes you appreciate everyone and everything you once had,
Covid-19 came in without warning
Deadly and unseen
Reconstructing everything,
We've had a lot of time to get to know our selves
Rebuild relationships, and bond with our families,
While the virus still spreads
Please just make sure you sanitize and keep your six feet.

Hidden Secrets

The perfect relationship
Catches me by surprise
One minute were laughing and cuddling
Now I'm reading text between you and another guy,
My body feels numb
I start to feel betrayed
Not believing my eyes
Or what I'm reading this day,
Though it was in the past
I can't help but to feel lied to
I wake you up with questions
Not knowing what you're about to do,
You become defensive
And it breaks my heart even more
Who is this man I'm starring at
I need answers before you reach the door,
I'm so confused
I don't even know who to reach out to
I need to vent, a listening ear
But I'm so embarrassed
So in tears I just sit there
My chest feels heavy
Its getting hard to breathe
I just want to know
Why did you do this to me?
I can't think straight

Though its getting very late
I can't close my eyes
I need to know if everything we built was based on lies,
I called the guy,
Yes I confronted your ex lover
I asked him if you two were undercover
He laughed it off then hung up the phone
I raced to your place,
Caught by surprise
You were shocked to see my face,
I guess I made it in time
You guys were already on a call
"Put him on speaker"
Tell him to confess it all!
He defends you
And says you're just friends,
"Dude get your girlfriend,
Why is she trippin?"
I know what I read
And I know what you said
You called him baby,
Told him you missed his touch
Straight men don't talk that way
It's okay to say you're gay!
Instead you play with my emotions

And leave my heart and mind confused
Now I'm a deep stuck in the headlights
I don't know what else to do,
I want to believe you and put this in the past
But I read the whole thread
A conversation that should've been dead
We waited five years for us to be together
No more social media chase,
You have me, I'm right here
In your face
I can't unsee the text
They just cloud my mind
One minute I love you
The next I feel like I'm wasting my time,
It been a long week,
Not one day at a time, but seven
I don't know if my man really loves me
Or if he's having an affair with Kevin.

Just Me

Most people judge me
Because of how I carry myself
I'm well spoken, well dressed
Though some days
I don't care that my hair's a mess,
I can wear Chanel or Old Navy
So don't scrooge up your face
And look at me like I'm crazy,
this generation likes Mary jane
I don't discriminate but we are not the same,
I'll have some Patron or Ciroc on ice
I like to play spades, but I don't know shit about dice,
I have a resting bitch face
But I know how to smile
I'm sweet but shy
So it may take a while,
I'm very opiniated so I smile the bullshit away
I'd rather laugh than fight
Or play music and have photoshoots at night,
I have my skeletons,

I've been hurt in the past
I've been a foster kid
I just don't broadcast what I did,
I've been abused,
The counselors did no good
I take detours through town
I've never hung out in any hoods
Chitterlings? What's that?
Some people would joke around
And say I'm not black,
I listen to Monica, Beyoncé, Luther and Taylor Swift
Don't judge me by the song I play
My emotions just vary based on the day,
Before you judge a book by it's cover
I'm misinterpreted and often called boogie
I'm humble and a sweetheart
Not cocky, I'm just me....

I know I broke your heart

Just give me a minute to explain
I hear the pain in your voice
When our son ask another mans name,
It's hard to tell you I've moved on
And found happiness with someone else
I know you're still in love with me
But I had to do what was good for myself,
We talked about rebuilding our relationship
And being a family for our son
But its been over a year now
And no progress has been done,
You want me to remain a single mom
While you're three states away
I'm young and beautiful
I want to get married some day,
I had a few dates here and there
But nothing serious enough
For us to discuss
Until I met this guy who made me smile without saying a word
Its like he knew my thoughts
And my prayers were finally heard,
We were inseparable
We spent a month together
Our son grew onto him

I knew I couldn't keep this secret forever,
Bonding with daddy
Turned into an interview,
Now I have to explain
Who's this guy I'm talking to,
I don't want you to hate me
I just didn't know how to tell you
We've been together since I was in high school
So the dating life I'm still getting used to,
I tried being honest
But I could tell I hurt you even more
I just want us to move on and be happy
It doesn't mean I'm trying to find our son a new daddy,
A week past
Not even a single text,
"Hey how's Jae?"
I get a response the next day
I don't see why you have to make things so tough
You don't want me, yet I can't date
I don't understand your selfish ways,
I apologize that I hurt you
And you had to find out from our son
I'm happy and deserve that too
Sorry I couldn't be the one.

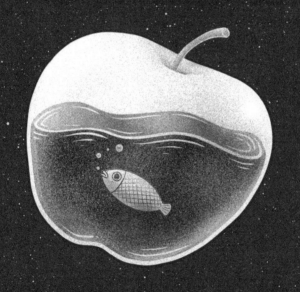

Stranded

You want to rebuild a bond
That's been broken far too long
You want me to act like you're a victim
And you've done nothing wrong,
It was supposed to be a night of fun,
A night of celebration
Instead you turned all of that
Into hate, deceit and devastation,
We left Mass as a party of two
Headed into the city
To celebrate the life of you,
Little did I know my world
Would be flipped upside down
Left in the middle of the city
And you never turned around!
I just reminded her that we were headed south
I guess since she's the parent, She knows it all
So I was told to watch my mouth
Because she's been driving
For as long as I've been alive
Expected to be quiet and pray that we survive
A heated argument,
Resulted in me standing in the cold rain
In the middle of City Island...
At 2am, everything looked strange,
I thought for sure I would see her head lights soon
Silly me, I was mistaken
She was racing back to town to see some dude,
I was left on the bridge
A few blocks from where they killed Junior

You don't understand
All the crazy shit I wanted to do when I finally saw her,
Every uber in the area was an older Italian guy
I phoned my aunt
Then all I could do is cry,
Who would leave their child two states away?
In the hood of New York,
I was definitely a pedophiles prey,
It took me six hours to finally get home
Its crazy how drugs expose feelings never shown
A night I never expected
One that could have turned very fatal and hectic,
Not a single text,
Or a, "hey did you make in home alright?"
I could've been floating in the Hudson River,
Headlines of New York City Times from that night
I would expect that from someone who wasn't blood
But the woman who birthed me
That bitch abandoned me for good,
I'm okay now and I've accepted the way things are
We can never repair this toxic relationship
I'll forever be scarred,
We can't spend holidays together,
Iyana can't fix this life
Stop fronting for Facebook
There's just way too much strife,
If I see you in Walmart
I might say, "hey"
But you'll never be my mother
For what you did that day.

I Want To Know You

Everyone always jokes about who my father is
Sometimes I go with the flow
Then I think of what my mother did,
I hear stories about how young my parents were
Not ready for that responsibility
but brave enough not to get rid of me,
my father calls me on my birthday
every year but on the wrong day,
when I tell him he's a week early
he always has something smart to say
don't even ask him to spell my name
he'll tell you that shit doesn't make sense
I just want to get to know him
And ask where he's been,
I see him more now that I'm older
But when were in the same room
My heart just gets colder,
We know nothing about one another
Not even our favorite colors
He's closer to the others
And a father to only my brothers,
But dad I'm here too
And I'm reaching out
Asking to get to know you,
I want to know the stranger that helped create me
I want to know your past, your history
Even your legacy,
I want you to know me too
My likes and dislikes

And how I aim to do everything right,
It may be too late because I'm grown now
Your baby's a teen
So you've lost hope on figuring us out,
But sometimes it helps
To know who your kids are
To know them inside out
And learn about every scar,
So that when people ask
"Hey how are your daughters?"
You won't shrug it off
Like you don't care to be bothered,
I want to know you dad
Let's sit down and talk
I want to know you dad
Before your too old and unable to walk,
I forgive you for your absence in life
I just want to move on
And try to make things right
Though there are seven of us
We all deserve to know the real you,
Can you tell me your dreams?
Or what influences you?
I want to know you dad
So my thoughts and late calls
Won't be all I've ever had.

A Cold September

Usually I'd be excited
Anxiously waiting for the fall
But since you've departed this world
I don't look forward to it at all,
I remember the car rides,
Hotdogs and beans grandma used to make
Trips to the gas station
And riding our bikes to the lake,
I remember playing in grandads' curly hair
Or faking sick at school
Just so I could stay there,
I remember sneaking into the Howard Johnson to go swimming
Even though we were told not to
The summers were crucial
What were we supposed to do?
We raced our bikes to Circuit City
Even stopped at Boston Market,
Boy we were rebellious
But always very cautious,
I just want you to know that it was very hard
Losing you both
Eighteen hours apart
I wouldn't process the hurt
Or prepare my broken heart,
I was in fifth grade
Going home to devastating news
You guys were my parents
I wasn't prepared for life after you!
I wasn't ready to say goodbye

Or hold your hand one last time
Grandad left his spirit In 110
Where he took his last breath
It hurts like hell
When you are trying to grieve two deaths,
I know that you are always with me
I can feel it in my soul,
I can sense it in the car
When I've had too much at the bar,
You always guide me safely
From point A to B
I know that all the family feud
Is pain for you to see
I try to remain neutral
And step away before I let them break me
I'd rather be isolated and alone
Protecting my energy in the comfort of my own home,
I would have loved for you to meet Jae
He's getting so big and advancing everyday,
I miss you so much it hurts to finish this poem
Tears fill the page
As I sniffle and hold back the rage,
Why were you taken from me so early in time?
I needed you guys longer
Some days I need your strength
So I can remain stronger,
I wear your anniversary dates forever in ink
Tattooed on my chest

Forever in memory
Stenciled the dates you were laid to rest,
You taught me to be strong, loving and caring
Be courageous and giving
Never stop achieving
And make a purpose for living,
I love you both
And I appreciate you in ways I can never express
I will always put my best foot forward
And give everything I attempt my best,
Please continue to watch over me and my son
I love you guys forever and a day
You're always my number one's!

~Dedicated~
Joe Wise & Lucille Wise
September 12, 2004 and September 13, 2004

Escaping Evil

Nana it's okay
You don't have to stay
You can always get out
This does not have to be what your last days are about,
I know that you're hurting
I see the pain in your eyes
Forced to fake a smile and live in disguise,
I hear the pain in your voice
I want you to know that you DO have a choice!
When you call every morning
I know it's because you're lonely again
You just want to talk
And feel like you have a real kin,
I hear the door slamming
And the verbal abuse
She's had a bad stroke
So none if this is what she's used to
Getting cursed out by her first born
Because she asked for a sweater
All they do is lock her away
Her mental health doesn't get better,
It breaks my heart to see them tear her apart
Family encourages her to go to a nursing home,
"I can't, she won't let me leave."
Forced to live with her daughter
But she's just evil and full of greed,
Locked away in a room,

She's paralyzed so she can't leave,
"Where's my grandma?"
"She's fine, let her be."
The family gathers outside for events
But I don't see your face,
I know you hear the excitement through the vents
Torn down and left in your grandsons' room all day
This isn't life Nana
"You don't have to live this way!"
Reports are filed
But she protects her daughter
Because of trauma and denial
She lives in fear and everyone can tell,
She doesn't want to be there
She feels like she's in hell
I want to help her see the light
And realize there is a way out
She's afraid to speak up
And living with doubt,
Scared to admit that she's dying of depression
Afraid to talk about what's done to her
Locked within four walls
Traumatized by her own daughter.

CPSIA information can be obtained
at www.ICGtesting.com
Printed in the USA
FSHW011818251020
75144FS